For
Tubby Toes, Hawthorn and Pteddy
Who all like picnics

The illustrator would like to thank
The Bethnal Green Museum of Childhood
and the Bear Museum, Petersfield
for the inspiration for many of the
bears portrayed in this book.

First published 1987 by
Blackie and Son Limited

This edition published 1992
Reprinted 1995 and 2002 by
Uplands Books
1 The Uplands, Maze Hill
St Leonards, E. Sussex TN38 0HL

Text of the song 'The Teddy Bears' Picnic'
Copyright © 1932 B. Feldman and Co. Ltd.
London WC2H 0LD
Reproduced by permission of
International Music Publications.

Illustrations copyright © 1987 Prue Theobalds

The moral right of the illustrator has been asserted

British Library Cataloguing in Publication Data
Kennedy, Jimmy
      The teddy bears' picnic.
      I. Title II. Theobalds, Prue
      823'. 914 (J) PZ7
      ISBN: 0-9512246-3-8 Hbk
      ISBN: 1-897951-46-9 Pbk

Yr 1

The Teddy Bears' Picnic

Pictures by
Prue Theobalds

Words by
by Jimmy Kennedy

UPLANDS BOOKS

If you go down in the woods today
You're sure of a big surprise.

If you go down in the woods today
You'd better go in disguise;

For ev'ry bear that ever there was
Will gather there for certain, because
Today's the day the Teddy Bears have
their picnic.

Ev'ry Teddy Bear who's been good
Is sure of a treat today.

There's lots of marvellous things to eat,

And wonderful games to play.

Beneath the trees where nobody sees
They'll hide and seek as long as they please,
'Cause that's the way the Teddy Bears have
their picnic.

If you go down in the woods today
You'd better not go alone.

It's lovely down in the woods today
But safer to stay at home.

For ev'ry Bear that ever there was

Will gather there for certain, because
Today's the day the Teddy Bears have their
picnic.

Picnic time for Teddy Bears,

The little Teddy Bears are having a lovely time today.
Watch them, catch them unawares
And see them picnic on their holiday.

See them gaily gad about,
They love to play and shout;
They never have any care.

At six o'clock their Mummies and Daddies
Will take them home to bed,
Because they're tired little Teddy Bears.